ALCESTIS

Borgo Press Books Edited & Translated by FRANK J. MORLOCK

Alcestis: A Play in Five Acts, by Philippe Quinault * *Anna Karenina: A Play in Five Acts*, by Edmond Guiraud, from Leo Tolstoy * *Anthony: A Play in Five Acts*, by Alexandre Dumas, Père * *Atys: A Play in Five Acts*, by Philippe Quinault * *The Boss Lady: A Play in Five Acts*, by Paul Féval, Père * *The Children of Captain Grant: A Play in Five Acts*, by Jules Verne & Adolphe d'Ennery * *Cleopatra: A Play in Five Acts*, by Victorien Sardou * *Crime and Punishment: A Play in Three Acts*, by Frank J. Morlock, from Fyodor Dostoyevsky * *Don Quixote: A Play in Three Acts*, by Victorien Sardou, from Miguel de Cervantes * *The Dream of a Summer Night: A Fantasy Play in Three Acts*, by Paul Meurice * *Falstaff: A Play in Four Acts*, by William Shakespeare, John Dennis, William Kendrick, & Frank J. Morlock * *The Idiot: A Play in Three Acts*, by Frank J. Morlock, from Fyodor Dostoyevsky * *Isis: A Play in Five Acts*, by Philippe Quinault * *Jesus of Nazareth: A Play in Three Acts*, by Paul Demasy * *The Jew of Venice: A Play in Five Acts*, by Ferdinand Dugué * *Joan of Arc: A Play in Five Acts*, by Charles Desnoyer * *The Lily of the Valley: A Play in Five Acts*, by Théodore Barrière & Arthur de Beauplan, from Honoré de Balzac * *Lord Byron in Venice: A Play in Three Acts*, by Jacques Ancelot * *Louis XIV and the Affair of the Poisons: A Play in Five Acts*, by Victorien Sardou * *The Man Who Saw the Devil: A Play in Two Acts*, by Gaston Leroux * *Mathias Sandorf: A Play in Three Acts*, by Jules Verne & William Busnach * *Michael Strogoff: A Play in Five Acts*, by Jules Verne & Adolphe d'Ennery * *Les Misérables: A Play in Two Acts*, by Victor Hugo, Paul Meurice, & Charles Victor Hugo * *Monte Cristo, Part One: A Play in Five Acts*, by Alexandre Dumas, Père * *Monte Cristo, Part Two: A Play in Five Acts*, by Alexandre Dumas, Père * *Monte Cristo, Part Three: A Play in Five Acts*, by Alexandre Dumas, Père * *Monte Cristo, Part Four: A Play in Five Acts*, by Alexandre Dumas, Père * *The Musketeers: A Play in Five Acts*, by Alexandre Dumas, Père * *The Mysteries of Paris: A Play in Five Acts*, by Eugène Sue & Prosper Dinaux * *Napoléon Bonaparte: A Play in Six Acts*, by Alexandre Dumas, Père * *Ninety-Three: A Play in Four Acts*, by Victor Hugo & Paul Meurice * *Notes from the Underground: A Play in Two Acts*, by Frank J. Morlock, from Fyodor Dostoyevsky * *Outrageous Women: Lady MacBeth and Other French Plays*, edited by Frank J. Morlock * *Peau de Chagrin: A Play in Five Acts*, by Louis Judicis, from Honoré de Balzac * *The Prisoner of the Bastille: A Play in Five Acts*, by Alexandre Dumas, Père * *A Raw Youth: A Play in Five Acts*, by Frank J. Morlock, from Fyodor Dostoyevsky * *Richard Darlington: A Play in Three Acts*, by Alexandre Dumas, Père * *The San Felice: A Play in Five Acts*, by Maurice Drack, from Alexander Dumas, Père * *Saul and David: A Play in Five Acts*, by Voltaire * *Shylock, the Merchant of Venice: A Play in Three Acts*, by Alfred de Vigny * *Socrates: A Play in Three Acts*, by Voltaire * *The Son of Porthos: A Play in Five Acts*, by Émile Blavet, from M. Paul Mahalin * *The Stendhal Hamlet Scenarios and Other Shakespearean Shorts from the French*, edited by Frank J. Morlock * *A Summer Night's Dream: A Play in Three Acts*, by Joseph-Bernard Rosier & Adolphe de Leuwen * *Urbain Grandier and the Devils of Loudon: A Play in Four Acts*, by Alexandre Dumas, Père * *The Voyage Through the Impossible: A Play in Three Acts*, by Jules Verne & Adolphe d'Ennery * *The Whites and the Blues: A Play in Five Acts*, by Alexandre Dumas, Père * *William Shakespeare: A Play in Six Acts*, by Ferdinand Dugué * *The Youth of the Musketeers: A Play in Five Acts*, by Alexandre Dumas, Père

ALCESTIS

A PLAY IN FIVE ACTS

by

Philippe Quinault

Translated and Adapted by Frank J. Morlock

THE BORGO PRESS

An Imprint of Wildside Press LLC

MMX

Copyright © 2003, 2010 by Frank J. Morlock

All rights reserved. No part of this book may be reproduced without the expressed written consent of the author. Professionals are warned that this material, being fully protected under the copyright laws of the United States of America, and all other countries of the Berne and Universal Copyright Convention, is subject to a royalty. All rights, including all forms of performance now existing or later invented, but not limited to professional, amateur, recording, motion picture, recitation, public reading, radio, television broadcasting, DVD, and Role Playing Games, and all rights of translation into foreign languages, are expressly reserved. Particular emphasis is placed on the question of readings, and all uses of these plays by educational institutions, permission for which must be secured in advance from the author's publisher, Wildside Press, 9710 Traville Gateway Dr. #234, Rockville, MD 20850 (phone 301-762-1305).

www.wildsidebooks.com

FIRST WILDSIDE EDITION

CONTENTS

Cast of Characters 7

Prologue 11

Act I 17

Act II 35

Act III 53

Act IV, Scene 1 67

Act IV, Scene 2 72

Act V 79

About the Editor 90

DEDICATION

To

TONY SMITH

CAST OF CHARACTERS

THE NYMPH OF THE SEINE

GLORY

FOLLOWERS OF GLORY

NYMPH OF THE TUILERIES

TROUPE OF NAIADS AND HAMADRYADS

THE NYMPH OF THE MARNE

TROUPE OF RIVER DIVINITIES

THE PLEASURES

CHORUS OF THESSALIANS

ALCIDAS, or HERCULES

LYCAS, confidant of Alcidas

STRATO, confidant of Lycomedes

CEPHISES, confidant of Alcestis

LYCOMEDES, brother of Thetis, and King of the Island of Scyros

PHERES, father of Admetus

ADMETUS, King of Thessaly

CLEANTES, Admetus' squire

ALCESTIS, princess of Iolchis

PAGES AND SERVANTS

TROUPE OF SEA DIVINITIES

THETIS, Nereid

FOUR AQUILONS

AEOLUS, king of winds

TROUPE OF LYCOMEDES' SOLDIERS

TROUPE OF THESSALIAN SOLDIERS

APOLLO

THE ARTS

TROUPE OF AFFLICTED WOMEN

TROUPE OF DESOLATE MEN

DIANA

MERCURY

CHARON

THE SHADES

PLUTO

PROSERPINE

THE SHADE OF ALCESTIS

SERVANTS OF PLUTO, singing dancing and flying

ALECTO, one of the Furies

CHORUS OF GREEKS

THE NINE MUSES

THE GAMES

TROUPE OF SHEPHERDS AND SHEPHERDESSES

TROUPE OF HERDSMEN

10 * *ALCESTIS*, BY PHILIPPE QUINAULT

PROLOGUE

The action of the Prologue takes place on the shores of the Seine, in the garden of the Tuileries.

The stage represents the palace and the garden of the Tuileries; the Nymph of the Seine appears, leaning on an urn in the midst of an alley of trees separated by fountains.

NYMPH OF THE SEINE:

Won't the hero that I am expecting come back?
Will I forever languish
In such a cruel expectation?
Won't the hero that I am expecting come back?
You no longer hear the bird sing,
You no longer see flowers spring up under our feet.
Won't the hero that I am expecting come back?
Growing grass
Seems to be dying.

Everything languishes with me in these alluring abodes.
Won't the hero that I am expecting come back?
Will I forever languish
In such a cruel expectation?
Won't the hero that I am expecting come back?
What rumor of war appalls me?
What divinity is going to descend down here?

(Glory appears in the midst of a shining palace that descends to the uproar of warlike harmony.)

NYMPH OF THE SEINE:

Alas! Superb Glory, alas!
Shouldn't you be satisfied?
Won't the hero that I am expecting come back?
He follows you only too much into the horror of battle;
Leave his triumphant valor in peace for a moment.
Won't the hero that I am expecting come back?
Will I forever languish
In such a cruel expectation?
Won't the hero that I am expecting come back?

GLORY:

Why so much grumbling? Nymph, your complaint is vain.

You cannot see the hero that you serve without me.
If his distance costs you so much pain,
He sufficiently compensates for the delights that you are losing.
See what he's making for you when Glory leads him,
See how his valor has subdued the Seine,
The proudest river that exists in the universe.

NYMPH OF THE SEINE:

One never sees here any more
So many imperfect decorations.
Ah! Come back to us our august master,
You will bring us back all our appeal.

GLORY:

He'll be back, and you ought to trust me.
I am carefully serving as his guide.
Since you see Glory,
Your hero is not far off.
He's letting the whole world catch its breath.
To fulfill his wishes, let's be in agreement here.

GLORY AND THE NYMPH OF THE SEINE:

How sweet it is to reconcile Glory and pleasures!

NYMPH OF THE SEINE:

Naiads, gods of forests, nymphs, let all assemble.
Let our singing be heard after so much sighing.

(The Nymph of the Tuileries comes forward with her troupe of nymphs; the trees open and reveal rustic divinities who play different instruments and the fountains change into Naiads who sing.)

CHORUS:

How sweet it is to reconcile
Glory and pleasures!

NYMPH OF THE TUILERIES:

Art agrees with nature
To serve love in these charming parts.
These waters which cause dreaming with such sweet murmurs,
These lawns where flowers form so many decorations,
These fields, these beds of green,
Everything is made for lovers.

(The Nymph of the Marne, companion of the Seine, comes to sing in the midst of a troupe of river divinities who express their joy by dancing.)

NYMPH OF THE MARNE:

The ocean rushes
To go on endlessly
To the end of its course.
So it is necessary for a heart to follow its inclination.
What is there that's more charming
Than the soft inclination of love?

GLORY AND THE NYMPH OF THE SEINE:

Let everything resound
Let all reply to our voices.

NYMPH OF THE TUILERIES:

Let all flower
In our gardens, in our woods.

NYMPH OF THE MARNE:

Let the songs of birds unite
With the sweet sound of oboes.

ALL TOGETHER:

Let everything resound,
Let all reply to our voices.
Let the songs of birds unite
With the sweet sound of oboes.

Let everything resound,
Let all answer to our voices.

(The rustic divinities and the nymphs form a general dance, while all the instruments and all the voices join in.)

ALL TOGETHER:

What savage heart
Doesn't get entangled here?
What savage heart
Doesn't feel love?
We are going to see the pleasures come back.
Let's not fail to make a sweet custom,
To laugh a bit is not less wise.
Ah! What a shame
To flee this shore!
Ah! What a shame
To lose a fine day!
We are going to see the pleasures come back.
To laugh a little is no less wise.
Come back, exiled pleasures,
Fly back from all sides, fly back.

(The pleasures fly in and come to prepare diversions.)

CURTAIN

ACT I

The action takes place is the city of Iolchis in Thessaly.

The stage represents a seaport in which is seen a great vessel prepared for a gallant celebration amidst several warships.

CHORUS OF THESSALIANS:

Live, live, happy spouses.

LYCAS:

Your dearest friend is wedding
The most charming princess in Greece.
Lord, when everyone is following them, why are you fleeing?

CHORUS OF THESSALIANS:

Live, live, happy spouses.

LYCAS:

You seem troubled by the shouts that are resounding!
When two happy lovers are uniting
Can the heart of great Alcidas be jealous?

CHORUS: Live, live, happy spouses.

LYCAS: Lord, you are sighing and keep silent!

ALCIDAS: Ah! Lycas! Let me depart swiftly.

LYCAS: What! This very day, to rush to leave!

ALCIDAS: I will waste my time rushing myself,
I will leave too late.
I don't intend to keep silent with you.
Alcestis is too adorable; she's pleased me too much;
Another is loved, nothing flatters my wishes.
It's over, Admetus is marrying her
And they're joining the two of them at this moment.
Ah! How a jealous soul
Endures a harsh torture!
I'm having trouble expressing myself.
Imagine, if you can,
How intense the horror is
To see the one you love

In the power of a happy rival.

LYCAS:

Is Love stronger than an indomitable hero?
The universe doesn't have a formidable monster
That you haven't been able to overcome.

ALCESTIS:

Hey! Do you think Love is less to be feared?
The greatest heart has its weakness.
I cannot save myself from the passion that urges me
To leave this fatal abode.
Against pleasant charms
Valor is without arms.
And it's only by fleeing that one can conquer love.

LYCAS:

You must force yourself at least to see the celebration
Which already appears ready in this port.
Your flight now would cause too great an uproar!
Delay it until midnight.

ALCIDAS:

Ah, Lycas! What a night! Ah! What a funereal night!

LYCAS:

For the remainder of the day, see Alcestis again.

ALCIDAS:

To see her again! Well! Let's delay my departure.
I told you well enough, I was leaving too late.
I am going to see her love a spouse who adores her.
I will see in their eyes a tender eagerness.
How dearly I am going to pay
For the pleasure of seeing her again!

(Strato enters.)

ALCIDAS, STRATO and LYCAS:

Love has many ills, but the greatest of all
Is the torture of being jealous.

(Alcidas leaves.)

STRATO:

Lycas, I need to speak to you briefly.

LYCAS:

What do you want? Speak, I'm listening to you.

STRATO:

We are friends for all times.
Cephises, you know, holds me under her sway.
You follow her steps everywhere; what do you intend?

LYCAS:

I intend to laugh.

STRATO:

Why do you want to disturb two hearts which are satisfied?

LYCAS:

I intend to laugh.
You can, if you like, get upset.
Each has his manner of loving;
Whoever wishes to sigh, sighs,
I intend to laugh.

STRATO:

I love, and I am loved; leave our love in peace.

LYCAS:

Nothing should alarm you. If it's really true she loves you

A rival rebuffed gives extreme pleasure.

STRATO:

A rival whoever he may be is always importunate.

LYCAS:

I see you love without rage.
You ought to behave this way.
Since Cephises knew how to please you,
Why don't you want her to please me, too?

STRATO:

What's the use of loving someone you must leave?
You cannot remain for long in this court.

LYCAS:

The less time one has to give to love,
The more it's necessary to profit from it.

STRATO:

I've loved for two years with fidelity,
Without vanity, I believe
That you ought not to be a rival to alarm me.

LYCAS:

I have novelty going for me.
In love that's a great charm.

STRATO:

Cephises has promised me a tender and constant heart.

LYCAS:

Cephises has promised me as much.

STRATO:

Ah! If I believed it! But you are not credible.

LYCAS:

Trust me, profit by a remaining friendship,
Employ some charitable advice
That I am giving you from pity.

STRATO:

The scorn of a theft
Must be a great enough evil
And it's a new outrage
To be pitied by a rival.
The faithless one is coming
To sing in the games which I'm preparing here.

LYCAS:

I'll leave you with her
All you need is to be better informed.

(Exit Lycas, enter Cephises.)

CEPHISES:

In this fine day, what somber mood
Makes you see a vexation?

STRATO:

It's that I am not amongst the number
Of satisfied lovers.

CEPHISES:

A bitter and scolding tone
Isn't very agreeable;
Anger doesn't advance
The affairs of a lover.

STRATO:

Lycas just made me understand
That I no longer have your heart, that he alone can pretend to it
And that you no longer see my love except with regrct.

CEPHISES:

Lycas is not very discreet.

STRATO:

Ah! I suspected indeed that he intended to surprise me.

CEPHISES:

Lycas is not very discreet
To have told my heart's secret.

STRATO:

What! So, it's really true? You don't even make an excuse!
You betray me like this, without even being ashamed!

CEPHISES:

You complain without reason.
Is it a betrayal
When one disabuses you?

STRATO:

How astonished I am to see your change!

CEPHISES:

If I change lovers
What do you find strange in it?
Is it a subject of astonishment

To see a girl who's changeable?

STRATO:

After two years spent in such sweet fetters,
Ought you ever take on a new chain?

CEPHISES:

Are you counting as nothing
Being faithful for two years?

STRATO:

By a sweet and deceitful hope,
Why did you entice me into such a tender love?
Did you need to give me your heart
Since you intended to take it back?

CEPHISES:

When I offered you my heart, it was in good faith.
What is preventing you from taking it back?
Is it my fault
If Lycas pleases me more than you?

STRATO:

Ingrate! Is this the reward of my constancy?

CEPHISES:

Try a little inconstancy.

It's you who were the first to teach me to entangle myself.
As a reward
I want to teach you to be changeable.

STRATO:

It's necessary to love forever.

CEPHISES:

It's necessary to change forever.

STRATO:

The sweetest loves are fulfilled loves.

CEPHISES:

New loves are the sweetest.

STRATO AND CEPHISES:

It's necessary to love forever.
It's necessary to change forever.

(Enter Lycomedes.)

LYCOMEDES:

Strato, give the order for them to get ready
To begin the celebration.

(Strato withdraws and Lycomedes speaks to Cephises.)

LYCOMEDES:

Finally, thanks to scorn, I taste the delight
Of feeling rest return to my heart.
The king of Thessaly was preferred over me,
And if for his glory they publish
That Apollo used to serve him as a shepherd,
I am king of Scyros, and Thetis is my sister.
I knew how to console myself for a marriage that outraged me.
I've arranged the games calmly.
How easily scorn removes
The Fetters of an ingrate beauty.
And, after a long slavery
How sweet it is to be free!

CEPHISES:

It's not always safe to believe appearances.
A heart really smitten is always touched.
It's not easily detached,
Nor as soon cured as one thinks.
And love is often hidden
Under a feigned indifference.

LYCOMEDES:

When one is without hope,
One is soon without love.
My rival has the preference.
The one I love is in his power,
I am losing all hope in one day.
When one is without hope,
One is soon without love.
The time's come for the celebration to begin,
Each is coming forward.
Let's prepare ourselves.

(Enter Admetus, Alcestis, Alcidas, Lycas, and the Chorus.)

CHORUS:

Live, live, happy spouses.

PHERES:

Enjoy the delights of
The bond that brings you together.

ADMETUS AND ALCESTIS:

When love and marriage agree so well together
Let the bonds they form be sweet!

CHORUS:

Live, live, happy spouses.

(Sea nymphs and tritons come to make a marine celebration, in which are mixed sailors and fishermen.)

TWO TRITONS:

Despite so many storms
And so many shipwrecks,
Each in his turn
Embarks with Love.
Wherever they lead him
Impassioned hearts
Envision the sea
Full of dangerous reefs,
But without some pain
They are never happy.
A faithful soul,
After torture,
Hopes for a fine day.
Despite so many storms
And so many shipwrecks,
Each in his turn
Embarks with Love.
A heart which delays
To enter the affair

Risks missing
The time to set sail.
A common soul
Is at first astonished.
The difficulty importunes him,
Calm makes him doze.
But what fortune
Is there without some effort?
Is it a business
Exempt from reversal?
A heart which delays
To enter the affair
Risks missing
The time to set sail.

CEPHISES:

(dressed as a divinity of the sea, sings in the midst of marine divinities, who reply to her)

Young hearts, let yourselves be captured;
The peril of waiting is dreary.
You will lose some happy moments
By trying to defend yourselves.
If love has its tortures,
It's the fault of lovers.

A SEA NYMPH SINGING WITH CEPHISES:

The more rebellious souls are,

The more cruel their pains.
Sweet and charming pleasures
Are the rewards of faithful hearts.
If love has its tortures,
It's the fault of lovers.

LYCOMEDES: (to Alcestis)

They are preparing for you
On my ship
A new diversion.

LYCOMEDES AND STRATO:

Come see what our celebration
Has that is the finest.

(Lycomedes escorts Alcestis onto his ship; Strato leads Cephises, and just as Admetus and Alcidas intend to pass, the bridge sinks into the sea.)

ADMETUS AND ALCIDAS:

God! The bridge is being swallowed by the water.

CHORUS OF THESSALIANS:

Ah! What funereal treason!

ALCESTIS AND CEPHISES:

Help! Help!

ALCIDAS:

Perfidy!

ADMETUS:

Alcestis!

ALCIDAS AND ADMETUS:

Let's leave this vain talk.
To the rescue! To the rescue!

(The Thessalians run to embark to follow Lycomedes.)

CHORUS OF THESSALIANS:

To the rescue, to the rescue!

THETIS: (emerging from the sea)

Unlucky spouses, fear my rage.
You are going to hasten the moment that must end your days.
It's Thetis that the sea reveres
And whom you see against you on her brother's side.
And you're running towards death.

ADMETUS (running to embark):

To the rescue! To the rescue!

THETIS:

Since they scorn my power,
Let unchained winds,
Let mutinous waves,
Arm themselves for my vengeance.

(Thetis returns to the sea, and the winds excite a storm which agitates the vessels which are prevented from pursuing Lycomedes.)

AEOLUS: (entering with Winds and Zephyrs)

Heaven protects heroes.
Go, Admetus. Go Alcidas.
The god who presides over gods
Is ordering me to calm the waves.
Go, pursue a perfidy.
Withdraw,
Enraged winds,
Return to your deep prisons
And let the softest zephyrs
Reign over the waves.

(The storm ceases, the Zephyrs fly and make the winds that are falling into the sea with the clouds they had raised, and the vessels of Alcidas and Admetus pursue Lycomedes.)

CURTAIN

ACT II

The stage represents the town of Scyros the principal city of the island.

CEPHISES:

Alcestis isn't coming any more, and we must wait.

STRATO:

What can she intend?
Why torture herself here so uselessly?
Her screams can't be heard,
Perhaps her husband perished in the waves
And we are at last in the island of Scyros.

CEPHISES:

You won't complain that I acted the same.
I've given you little trouble;
You see I follow your steps.

STRATO:

You now hope to dissimulate an intense rage.

CEPHISES:

And if I told you it was you alone that I loved?

STRATO:

You would say it in vain: I wouldn't believe you.

CEPHISES:

Trust me, if I pretended to change,
It was only to entice you the more.
A rival isn't useless.
He reawakens passion and the concerns of a lover.
An easy conquest
Gives little eagerness,
And calm love
Easily dozes off.

STRATO:

No, no, don't tempt me with a second trick.
I see more clearly than you think.
People excuse a lover at first that abused them.
But the stupidity of allowing oneself to be twice deceived
Has no excuse.

CEPHISES:

Is there no way to appease your rage?

STRATO:

Agree to marry me, and without delay.

CEPHISES:

Such a great affair
Is not finished promptly;
A marriage delayed
Is only more charming.

STRATO:

A marriage that can please
Doesn't cost.
And it's a bond soon formed.
There's nothing easier than to make
A spouse out of a beloved lover.

CEPHISES:

I love you with a sincere love.
And, if necessary,
I am offering to swear an oath to you.

STRATO:

Amusing, amusing.

CEPHISES:

The unjust kidnapping of Alcestis
Is attracting a funereal war to these parts.
The bravest of the Greeks are arming to help her.
In the midst of screams and tears
Marriage has few charms.
The terrifying uproar of arms
Really shocks love.

STRATO:

Talk, talk, talk.
All you have to do is marry me to remove all Umbrage from me.
Why put it off longer,
What's the use of all these manners?

CEPHISES:

Restore me my freedom, so as to marry me without fear.
A forced marriage
Is a bad way to end your suspicions.

STRATO:

Sing, sing, sing.

(Lycomedes enters with Alcestis and soldiers.)

LYCOMEDES:

Come, come, the complaint is very vain.

ALCESTIS:

Ah! What inhumane harshness!

LYCOMEDES:

Go on, I'm deaf to your screams.
I'm avenging myself for your scorn.

ALCESTIS:

What! You will be inexorable!

LYCOMEDES:

Cruel one! You've taught me
To become pitiless.

ALCESTIS:

Is it thus that love knew how to move you?
Is this the way your soul is softened for me?

LYCOMEDES:

Love changes into fury
When it is in despair.
Since I am losing all hope,
I intend to despair my rival in his turn,

And the delights of vengeance
Have what's needed to console the harshness of Love.

ALCESTIS:

See the sorrow that overwhelms me.

LYCOMEDES:

You observed my sorrow without pity.
You made me miserable,
You will share my misfortune.

ALCESTIS:

Admetus had my heart from my most tender childhood.
We didn't know love or its power
When a fatal bond came to enchain us.
It's not a great offense
To refuse a heart which is no longer free to be Given.

LYCOMEDES:

Is it for lovers in despair
To be obliged to examine everything?
No, I cannot forgive you
For having known how to please me too well.
What your funereal allures have cost me!

They've put in my heart a cruel flame.
They've torn from my soul
Innocence and peace.
No, ingrate! No, inhuman one!
No, whatever may be your pain
No, I will never free you
For all the wrongs you've done me.

STRATO:

Here's the enemy advancing
Speedily.

LYCOMEDES:

Let's prepare
To defend ourselves.

ALCESTIS:

Ah! Cruel! You won't spare yourself
The blood that's going to be shed.

LYCOMEDES AND SOLDIERS:

Let's all perish
Rather than surrender.

(Lycomedes forces Alcestis into the town. Cephises follows her and the soldiers of Lycomedes shut the gate of the town as soon as they have entered.)

(Admetus, Alcidas, Lycas and besieging soldiers enter.)

ADMETUS AND ALCIDAS:

March, march, march.
Come closer, friends, come closer.
March, march, march.
Let's hasten to punish traitors.
Let's become masters
Of the walls they are hidden in.
March, march, march.

LYCOMEDES: (on the ramparts)

Don't expect to surprise us.
Come, we are going to wait for you.
We are doing all our duty
To give you a fine reception.

STRATO AND THE BESIEGED SOLDIERS:

We are doing all our duty
To give you a fine reception.

ADMETUS:

Perfidious one, avoid a funereal fate.
You'll be forgiven for everything, if you will return

Alcestis.

LYCOMEDES:

If necessary, I prefer to die
Than to give up this object full of charms.

ADMETUS AND ALCIDAS:

To the assault, to the assault.

LYCOMEDES AND STRATO:

To arms, to arms.

THE BESIEGERS:

To the assault, to the assault.

THE BESIEGED:

To arms, to arms.

ADMETUS, ALCIDAS, and LYCOMEDES:

Rally to me, companions, rally to me.

ADMETUS AND LYCOMEDES:

Help me: follow your king.

ALCIDAS:

It's Alcidas

Who leads you.

ADMETUS, ALCIDAS, AND LYCOMEDES:

Rally to me, companions, rally to me.

(They bring forward the battering rams and other machines of war to beat in the place.)

ALL TOGETHER:

Give, give, everywhere.

THE BESIEGERS:

Let each desire to battle.
Let them beat down
The towers and the ramparts.

ALL TOGETHER:

Give, give, everywhere.

THE BESIEGED:

Let the enemies fall
In disorder under the terrifying hail
Of our arrows and our darts.

ALL:

Give, give, everywhere.
Courage, courage, courage.

They are ours, they are ours.

ALCIDAS:

It's no use arguing any further
I am going to open a passage.
Everyone follow me, everyone follow me.

ALL TOGETHER:

Courage, courage, courage.
They are ours, they are ours.

(The besieged, seeing their ramparts half overthrown and the gate of the town forced in, make a last effort by a sortie to repel the besiegers.)

THE BESIEGERS:

Let's finish carrying the place.
The enemy is beginning to fold.
To work, to work, to work.

THE BESIEGED: (surrendering their arms)

Quarter, quarter, quarter.

THE BESIEGERS:

The city is taken.

THE BESIEGED:

Quarter, quarter, quarter.

LYCAS: (knocking down Strato)

You must surrender Cephises.

STRATO:

I am your prisoner.
Quarter, quarter, quarter.

PHERES: (armed and walking with difficulty)

Courage, children, I am with you!
My arm is going to second your blows.
Why, it's already done, and they've taken the city.
The weakness of age delayed my steps.
Valor has become useless
When strength doesn't answer.
How slow age is,
The efforts that it makes
Are always impotent.
It's a very heavy burden
To be eighty years old

ALCIDAS:

Return to your son this adorable princess.

PHERES:

That gift will be even sweeter from your hand.

ALCIDAS:

Go on, go on, give her to her happy spouse.

ALCESTIS:

Everything is subdued; the war ceases.
Lord, why don't you let me go?
What new care imposes on you?

ALCIDAS:

You have nothing to fear,
I am going to seek tyrants to overthrow elsewhere.

ALCESTIS:

The bonds of a pressing friendship
Won't delay your impatient soul
And glory must always carry you off.

ALCIDAS:

Beware, indeed, of stopping me.

ALCESTIS:

It's your triumphant valor
That makes the fate we are going to enjoy charm-

ing.
A friend such as you
Augments the sweetness to be felt.
Will you leave us so soon?

ALCIDAS:

Beware, indeed, of stopping me.
Release me, let me flee a charm that enchants me.
No, all my virtue is not powerful enough
To answer for resisting it.
No, yet once more, too charming princess,
Beware, indeed, of stopping me

ALCESTIS, PHERES, CEPHISES:

Let's promptly find Admetus.

ALCESTIS:

Can one seek the person one loves
With too much eagerness?
When love is intense,
The least separation
Is a cruel torturer.

ALCESTIS, PHERES AND CEPHISES:

Let's promptly find Admetus.

(Admetus enters supported by Cleantes; he's

wounded.)

ALCESTIS:

O gods! What a funereal spectacle!

CLEANTES:

The chief of our enemies, dying and defeated,
In his expiring rage has done all he was able.
The king has just been wounded.

ADMETUS:

I am dying, charming Alcestis.
My fate is sweet enough
Because I am dying for you.

ALCESTIS:

It's to see you die that heaven is delivering me ?

ADMETUS:

I would have been too lucky to live
With the name of your spouse.
My fate is sweet enough
Because I am dying for you.

ALCESTIS:

Is this the marriage so sweet, so full of attractions,
That promised us so many charms?

Must the blind fate of arms so soon
Sever the beautiful fetters by a terrifying death?
Is this the marriage so sweet, so full of attractions,
That promised us so many charms?

ADMETUS:

Beautiful Alcestis, don't weep.
All my blood is not worth your tears.

ALCESTIS:

Is this the marriage so sweet, so full of attractions,
That promised us so many charms?

ADMETUS:

Alcestis, you're weeping.

ALCESTIS:

Admetus, you're dying.

ADMETUS AND ALCESTIS:

Alcestis, you're weeping.
Admetus, you're dying.

ALCESTIS:

Can heaven allow
The hearts of Alcestis and Admetus
To be separated like this?

ADMETUS AND ALCESTIS:

Alcestis, you're weeping.
Admetus, you're dying.

(Apollo, and the Arts appear.)

APOLLO: (surrounded by the Arts)

Today's light ought to ravish you.
It's the only way to prolong your fate.
Destiny promised me to return you to life
If someone else for you would offer themselves to die.
Recognize that if someone loves you perfectly,
Their death would have an immortal glory as its reward.
To commemorate their memory
The arts are going to raise a stately monument.

(The Arts who surround Apollo, separate themselves from different clouds and descend to erect a superb monument, as Apollo flies off.)

CURTAIN

ACT III

The stage represents a great monument erected by the Arts. An empty altar appears in the middle to be used to bear the image of the person who will sacrifice himself for Admetus.

ALCESTIS:

Ah! Why will you separate us?
Eh! At least wait for death to separate us.
Cruel ones! What barbarous pity
Urges you to snatch Alcestis from her spouse?
Ah! Why are you separating us?

PHERES AND CEPHISES:

The more your dying spouse sees love and attractions,
The more the life he's losing makes him envious.
These are the delights of life
That make death horrible.

ALCESTIS:

The Arts have not yet finished their work.
This altar must bear the glorious image
That will signal his faith
By dying to save his king.
The prize of a glorious immortality,
Can't it reach a great heart?
Mustn't the most beautiful death
Not cause fear?
What's the use of an importune crowd
With which kings are embarrassed?
Fortune's fatal blow
Separates the most eager.

ALCESTIS, PHERES, AND CEPHISES:

Of the many friends Admetus had
Not one comes to aid him.
Whatever honor they are promised,
They let him die.

PHERES:

I love my son, I made him king;
To prolong his fate, I will die without terror.
If I could offer life worthy of envy.
I have no more than a remainder of life.
It's nothing for Admetus, it's much for me.

CEPHISES:

The most dazzling honors
Vainly promise to follow us into the tomb.
Death is terrifying at all times.
But can one renounce living
If one has lived only fifteen years?

ALCESTIS:

Each is satisfied with the excuses he gives.
Still no one is to be seen
Who, to save Alcestis, dares to give up life.
Duty, friendship, blood, all abandon him.
He has no hope left except in love.

(Exit Alcestis.)

PHERES:

Let's look at my son again; let's go, let's hasten our steps.
His eyes are going to be covered in eternal shadows.

CHORUS:

Alas! Alas! Alas!

PHERES:

What shouts! What funereal complaints!

CHORUS:

Alas! Alas! Alas!

PHERES:

Where are you going, Cleantes? Stay.

CLEANTES:

Alas! Alas!
The king is reaching his last hour.
He's weakening; he must die.
And I am coming to weep at his death.
Alas! Alas!

CHORUS:

Alas! Alas! Alas!

PHERES:

They pity him; all the world weeps,
But our tears are not saving him.
Alas! Alas!

CHORUS:

Alas! Alas! Alas!

(Admetus enters.)

CHORUS:

O too lucky Admetus!
How beautiful your fate is!

PHERES AND CLEANTES:

What change! What new uproar!

CHORUS:

O too lucky Admetus!
How beautiful your fate is!

PHERES AND CLEANTES: (seeing Admetus cured)

The effort of perfect friendship
Saved him from the tomb.

PHERES: (embracing Admetus)

O too lucky Admetus!
How beautiful your fate is!

CHORUS:

O too lucky Admetus!
How beautiful your fate is.

ADMETUS:

Let a stately funeral

Forever celebrate
The generous effort
Of the person who snatched me form death.
Alcestis will have no further alarms.
I will see her charming eyes again,
Those I've caused so many tears.
How many charms has life
For happy lovers!
Finish up, gods of Arts: let's see the image
Which must eternalize the grandeur of courage
Of the one who sacrificed himself for me!
Don't delay any longer.
Heaven! O heaven! What is it I see?

(The altar opens and the image of Alcestis enters with its breast pierced.)

CEPHISES: (running in)

Alcestis is dead.

ADMETUS:

Alcestis is dead!

CHORUS:

Alcestis is dead.

CEPHISES:

Alcestis has satisfied the wrath of the Parcae.
Your tomb is opening; she's descending into it for you.
She herself wanted to shut the gate before you.
Alcestis is dead.

ADMETUS:

Alcestis is dead.

CHORUS:

Alcestis is dead.

CEPHISES:

I ran, but much too late, to stop her blows.
Never in favor of a spouse,
Will you see a passion so strong.
Alcestis is dead.

ADMETUS:

Alcestis is dead.

CHORUS:

Alcestis is dead!

CEPHISES:

Subjects, friends, relatives, all abandoned you.
Over the strongest rights, over the softest fetters.
Love, tender love, carried her away.
Alcestis is dead.

ADMETUS:

Alcestis is dead.

ADMETUS:

Alcestis is dead.

CHORUS:

Alcestis is dead.

(Admetus falls overcome with sorrow into the arms of his followers.)

(Enter a Troupe of Afflicted Women, and a Troupe of Desolated Men bringing flowers and all the ornaments that are employed to decorate Alcestis.)

ALL TOGETHER:

Let's compose the most lugubrious songs
And the most touching regrets.

AN AFFLICTED WOMAN:

Death, barbarous death,
Is destroying today a thousand attractions.
Alas! What a victim!
Was there ever such beauty—and so rare!
Death, barbarous death,
Is destroying today a thousand attractions.

A DESOLATED MAN:

Alcestis, so young and so beautiful,
Rushes to hurl herself into eternal night.
To save the one she loves, she's lost her life.

CHORUS:

O too perfect model
Of a faithful spouse!
O too perfect model
Of true love!

AN AFFLICTED WOMAN:

Let our zeal be divided.
Let some, with their songs, celebrate her courage.
Let others, with their wails, deplore her misfortunes.

CHORUS:

Let's pay homage
To her image.
Let's cast flowers.
Let's pour tears.

AN AFFLICTED WOMAN:

Alcestis, the charming Alcestis,
The faithful Alcestis, is no more.

CHORUS:

Alcestis, the charming Alcestis,
The faithful Alcestis, is no more.

AN AFFLICTED WOMAN:

So many beauties, so many virtues,
Deserve a less funereal fate.

CHORUS:

Alcestis, the charming Alcestis,
The Faithful Alcestis, is no more.

(A transport of sorrow seizes the two afflicted troupes; one group tears their clothes, the other pulls out their hair, and each breaks at the foot of Alcestis' image the ornaments they carried by hand.)

CHORUS:

Break, let's break the sad remains
Of these superfluous decorations.
Let our tears, let our wails, renew endlessly.
Let's go bring everywhere the sorrow that weighs on us.

(Exit the Chorus.)

ADMETUS: (awakening from his faint and seeing himself disarmed)

Without Alcestis, without her attractions,
Do you believe that I can go on living?
Let me rush to Death
That my cherished Alcestis is delivering herself to.
Without Alcestis, without her attractions,
Do you believe that I can go on living?
She died for me, alas!
Why prevent me from following her?
Without Alcestis, without her attractions,
Do you think that I can live?

ALCIDAS: (entering)

You see me stopped on the point of departure
By the sad clamors that are heard resounding.

ADMETUS:

Alcestis is dying for me from an intense love.
I will never again see the eyes that charmed me!
Alas! I've lost what I love
For having been loved too much.

ALCIDAS:

I love Alcestis: it's time to no longer deny it.
She's dying: your love no longer has anything to expect.
Admetus, surrender to me the beauty you are losing.
I undertake to descend to the palace of Pluto;
I will go to the depth of hell
To force Death to give her to me.

ADMETUS:

I will again see those beautiful eyes!
Go, Alcidas, go, return glorious!
Get Alcestis to follow you.
The son of the most powerful of gods
Is more worthy than I of the blessing
Of which they are depriving me.
Go, go, don't delay further,
Snatch Alcestis from Death
And bring to life her fugitive shade.

Let her live for you with all her attractions.
Admetus is very happy, so long as Alcestis is living

PHERES, CEPHISES, AND CLEANTES:

Go, go, don't delay further,
Snatch Alcestis from death.

(Enter Diana and Mercury. The moon appears; its globe opens and Diana is seen on a shining cloud.)

DIANA:

The god to whom you owe birth
Is obliging all the gods to be joined
In favor of so fine a plan.
I am coming to offer you my assistance
And Mercury is coming forward
To open a new passage to hell for you.

(Mercury comes flying in to strike the earth with his caduceus; hell opens and Alcidas descends.)

CURTAIN

66 * *Alcestis*, by Philippe Quinault

ACT IV

Scene 1

The stage represents the river Acheron and its somber shores.

CHARON:

Sooner or later you must pass,
Pass in my barge.
Young and old come here
As the Parcae please.
Without distinction they are received,
The shepherd and the monarch.
Sooner or later you must pass,
Pass on my barge.
You who wish to pass, come wandering Manes,
Come, come forward, sad shades,
Pay the tribute that I take
Or return to wander these somber shores.

THE SHADES:

Pass me, Charon, pass me.

CHARON:

First off let them satisfy me.
You must pay for the cares of one so painfully employed.

THE SHADES:

Pass me, Charon, pass me.

(Charon lets the shades who have paid him enter his barge.)

CHARON:

Gimme, pass; gimme, pass.
Stay, you.
You've got nothing, got to drive you off.

A REBUFFED SHADE:

A shade clings so little to rank.

CHARON:

Either pay, or go away.

SHADE:

Mercy, pity, don't rebuke me.

CHARON:

There's no pity down here.
And Charon has no mercy.

SHADE:

Alas! Charon, alas! Alas!

CHARON:

Wail alas! As much as you like.
Nothing for nothing; it's a law followed everywhere.
Empty hands are without appeal.
It's not enough to pay in life,
You must still pay further in death.

SHADE: (as he withdraws)

Alas! Charon, alas! Alas!

CHARON:

It doesn't bother me much that he wails.
Alas! Charon, alas! Alas!
You must still pay further in death.

ALCIDAS: (leaping into the barge)

Get out, shades, give me room,
You will pass another time.

(The shades flee.)

CHARON:

Ah! My barge can't endure such a great weight!

ALCIDAS:

Let's go, I have to pass.

CHARON:

Withdraw from here, mortal.
Irritated Hell will punish your audacity.

ALCIDAS:

Pass me, without so much ceremony.

CHARON:

The water is reaching us, my barge is breaking.

ALCIDAS:

Get moving, row, hurry up, get it over with.

CHARON:

We're sinking

ALCIDAS:

Pass, pass.

CURTAIN or BLACKOUT

ACT IV

Scene 2

The scene changes and represents the palace of Pluto.

PLUTO: (on his throne)

Receive the just rewards of your faithful love,
May your new destiny be forever happy.
Begin to taste the eternal delight
Of a profound peace.

FOLLOWERS OF PLUTO:

Begin to taste the eternal delight
Of a profound peace.

PROSERPINE: (at Pluto's side)

Pluto's spouse will keep you beside her.
All your wishes will be fulfilled.

FOLLOWERS OF PLUTO:

Begin to taste the eternal delight
Of a profound peace.

PLUTO AND PROSERPINE:

In favor of such a beautiful shade,
Let Hell reveal all its attractions.

(The followers of Pluto rejoice at the arrival of Alcestis in Hell with a sort of celebration.)

THE FOLLOWERS OF PLUTO:

In favor of such a beautiful shade,
Let Hell reveal all its attractions.
All mortals must appear here.
They're born
Only to die
From a hundred ills death delivers;
Those who seek to live
Are seeking only to suffer.
Come all to our somber shores.
The rest you want
Doesn't have sway
Except in the abodes of the dead.
Each comes down here to find a place,
Endlessly they come here,
Never do they leave.

For all it's a necessary law.
The effort that they make
Is only a vain effort.
Is it wise
To flee this passage?
It's a storm
That leads to port.
Endlessly they come here,
Never do they leave.
All the charms
Complaints, wails, tears,
All are without arms
Against Death.
Each comes down here to find a place,
Endlessly they come here,
Never do they leave.

ALECTO: (entering)

Leave, leave these games; think of protecting yourself.
Let's unite our efforts against an audacious man.
The son of Jupiter has just descended here.
Alone, he dares to attack the whole empire of Death.

PLUTO:

Let this bold one be stopped

Arm yourselves, friends, arm yourselves.
Let them unchain Cerberus.
Run everyone, run everyone.

(The baying of Cerberus is heard.)

ALECTO:

His arm beats down all it strikes.
Everything gives way to his horrible blows,
Nothing can resist him, nothing can escape him.

(Alcidas enters.)

PLUTO: (seeing Alcidas who enchains Cerberus)

Insolent! Do you brave my wrath to this degree?
What unjust audacity entices you
To disturb the peace of these parts?

ALCIDAS:

I was born to subdue the rage
Of the most furious monsters!

PLUTO:

Is it the jealous god who hurls thunder
Who obliges you to bring war
To the center of the universe?
He holds under his sway heaven and earth.
Does he still intend to ravish the Empire of Hell?

ALCIDAS:

No, Pluto, reign in peace, enjoy your share.
I'm coming to seek Alcestis in this frightful abode.
Permit me to give her life.
I want nothing more.
If it does you outrage
To forcefully enter your court,
Pardon my courage
And pity my love.

PROSERPINE:

A great heart can accomplish anything when it loves.
All must give way to its efforts.
It's a decree of fate
That intense love
Be much stronger
Than Death.

PLUTO:

Hell, Pluto himself,
All must be in agreement,
That intense love
Be much stronger
Than Death.

FOLLOWERS OF PLUTO:

It's necessary that intense love
Be much stronger
Than Death.

PLUTO:

Let the shade of Alcestis leave to receive life.

(Pluto gives a blow of his trident and makes his chariot appear.)

Both of you take your place in the chariot that serves me.
Let it take you at your wishes' pleasure.
Leave, the roads are open.
Let a flying escort
Lead you through
The dark vapors of hell.

(Alcidas and the shade of Alcestis place themselves in the chariot of Pluto which carries them off escorted by a flying troupe of the followers of Apollo.)

CURTAIN

ACT V

The stage represents a triumphal arch in the midst of two amphitheatres, where a multitude of different people from Greece are visible, assembled to receive Alcidas triumphing over Hell.

ADMETUS:

Alcidas is the conqueror of death,
Hell cannot resist him.
He's bringing back Alcestis, living.
Let each sing.
Alcidas is the conqueror of death,
Hell cannot resist him.

CHORUS: (on the triumphal arch and in the amphitheatre)

Alcidas is the conqueror of death,
Hell cannot resist him.

ADMETUS:

What secret sorrow
Tears my uneasy soul
And trembles for my love!
Alcestis sees light again,
But it's for someone other than Admetus.

CHORUS:

Alcidas is the conqueror of death,
Hell cannot resist him.

ADMETUS:

Ah! At least let's hide my sorrow!
Alcestis is attracting pleasures to these parts.
I ought to blush for my weakness.
What shame must my heart mingle with sighs
Before so many shouts of glee!

CHORUS:

Alcidas is the conqueror of Death,
Hell cannot resist him.

ADMETUS:

With an impatient passion
Let's run and outrun his steps.
He's bringing Alcestis living.

Let each sing.

ADMETUS AND THE CHORUS:

Alcidas is the conqueror of Death,
Hell cannot resist him.

(Exit Admetus and the Chorus. From a different direction enter Lycas with Strato enchained.)

STRATO:

Won't you release me from the chain that overwhelms me
On this day destined for so many pleasant games?
Ah, how harsh it is
To be the only wretch
When all the world is seen to be happy!

LYCAS: (freeing Strato)

Today, as Alcidas brings
Alcestis from Hell,
I intend to put an end to your pain.
Bear no other fetters
Than those with which Love enchains us.

STRATO AND LYCAS:

Bear no other fetters
Than those with which Love enchains us.

ALCESTIS, BY PHILIPPE QUINAULT * 81

(Cephises enters)

Look, Cephises, see which one of us
Must render your fate most sweet
And at last end our quarrels.

LYCAS:

My love will be eternal.

STRATO:

My heart will never be jealous.

LYCAS AND STRATO:

From two faithful lovers
Choose a lucky spouse.

CEPHISES:

I have no choice to make.
Let's speak of love and of pleasing,
And let's live always in peace.
Marriage destroys tenderness;
It deprives love of its allures.
If you want to love endlessly
Lovers, never marry.

CEPHISES, LYCAS, AND STRATO:

Marriage destroys tenderness;

It deprives love of its allures.
If you want to love endlessly
Lovers, never marry.

CEPHISES:

Let's take part in the distractions of a dazzling joy.
Let each sing.

ALL TOGETHER:

Alcidas is conqueror of Death,
Hell cannot resist him.
He's bringing back Alcestis, living.
Let each sing.
Alcidas is conqueror of Death,
Hell cannot resist him.

(Enter Alcidas, Alcestis, Admetus, Pheres, and Cleantes.)

ALCIDAS:

For such a beautiful victory,
Could one have undertaken too much?
Ah! How sweet it is to rush to glory
When love must give the reward!
You deflect your eyes! I find you insensitive!
Admetus alone has your softest glances.

ALCESTIS:

I'm doing what I possibly can
To only look at you.

ALCIDAS:

You must follow my desire;
It's because of me you are living.

ALCESTIS:

I haven't been able to resume living
Without resuming my love.

ALCIDAS:

Admetus, in my favor, has himself given you up.

ADMETUS:

Alcidas alone could snatch you from death.
Alcestis, you live, I see your allures again.
Have I paid too much for this intense tenderness?

ADMETUS AND ALCESTIS:

Ah! What won't you do
To save the one you love!

ALCIDAS:

The two of you sigh of your desires at your pleas-

ure?
Is this the way you keep your word to me?

ADMETUS AND ALCESTIS:

Pardon our last sighs.
From an unfortunate love that must be sacrificed to you,
We mustn't see each other any more.
On some one else than you my destiny must depend.
Necessarily, in great hearts, the most tender love
Must be the victim of duty.
We mustn't see each other any more.

(Admetus withdraws, and Alcestis offers his hand to Alcidas, who stops Admetus and gives her Alcestis hand.)

ALCIDAS:

No, you mustn't think
That a conqueror of tyrants may be a tyrant in his turn.
Over Hell, over Death, I bear the victory.
All that is lacking to my glory
Is to triumph over Love.

ADMETUS AND ALCESTIS:

Ah! What extreme glory!
What a heroic effort!
The conqueror of Death
Triumphs over himself.

(Apollo descends in a dazzling palace in the midst of Muses and Games that he brings to take part in the joy of Admetus and Alcestis and to celebrate the triumph of Alcidas.)

APOLLO:

The Muses and Games rush to descend;
Apollo is escorting them to these pleasant parts.
You that I've taken care to teach
To sing your love in the most tender tone,
Sing, sing, and let our songs
Reach right up to heaven.

(A troupe of shepherds and shepherdesses and a troupe of herdsmen, one of which sings and the other dances, by order of Apollo, to contribute to the rejoicing.)

CHORUS OF MUSES, THESSALIANS, AND SHEPHERDS: (singing together)

Sing, sing, and let our songs

Reach right up to heaven.

STRATO: (singing in the midst of dancing herdsmen)

What's the use
Of so much reason
In fine times?
What's the good
Of so much reason
Out of season?
Whoever fears the danger
Of being entangled
Is lacking in courage.
Everything laughs for lovers;
Charming games
Are their share.
Soon, soon, soon, we will be satisfied.
There comes a time when
We are too wise.

CEPHISES: (singing in the midst of dancing shepherds and shepherdesses)

It's the season to love
When one knows how to please;
It's the season to love
When one knows how to charm.
The most beautiful of our days won't last,

The fate of beauty ought to alarm us,
Our fields have no flowers more transient.
It's the season to love
When one knows how to please;
It's the season to love
When one knows how to charm.
A bit of love is necessary.
It's never too soon to be inflamed.
Were we given a heart to do nothing with it?
It's the season to love
When one knows how to please;
It's the season to love
When one knows how to charm.

(The troupe of shepherds dances with the troupe of herdsmen. The choruses answer each other and finally they join altogether.)

THE CHORUSES:

Triumph, generous Alcidas,
Love in peace, happy spouses,
Glory forever.
Let endless love guide you.
Enjoy forever pleasure of the most delightful sort.
Triumph, generous Alcidas.
Love in peace, happy spouses.

(Apollo flies with the games.)

CURTAIN

ABOUT FRANK J. MORLOCK

FRANK J. MORLOCK has written and translated many plays since retiring from the legal profession in 1992. His translations have also appeared on Project Gutenberg, the Alexandre Dumas Père web page, Literature in the Age of Napoléon, Infinite Artistries.com, and Munsey's (formerly Blackmask). In 2006 he received an award from the North American Jules Verne Society for his translations of Verne's plays. He lives and works in México.

www.ingramcontent.com/pod-product-compliance
Lightning Source LLC
LaVergne TN
LVHW011215080426
835508LV00007B/799